TABLE OF CONTENTS

INTRODUCTION

Let's face it -- we are all busy. The time when we could plan a full-course meal nightly has become a thing of the past. It is too easy to stop off at a fast food place on the way home from work or grab a quick snack on the way to an activity. We rarely have time to sit down and think of meals...let alone make them.

Oh sure, most people will try to make them. We follow the quick tips, we plan ahead, we thaw that meat, and we gather up as many 20-minute recipes as we can find. However, it doesn't quite seem to work. Let's face it, those "quick" 20-minute meals are never made in 20 minutes, and the quick tips don't help much either.

It may seem hopeless to have high quality, tasty meals with very little effort. But that is what this book offers you. **It takes two simple tools -- a slow cooker and an afternoon for prep work. If you can manage to have both, even one Sunday afternoon a month, you can have a homemade meal every day of the week with little effort.**

How do we do this? Well, the answer is simple. Slow cooker recipes can be prepped weeks ahead of time in just a few hours and frozen. All you need is one afternoon to cut up the meats and vegetables and store them into freezer bags. Then you can simply freeze the foods so they are ready when you are.

The meals presented here are rich in flavor and will please even the pickiest of eaters. To make them, after prepping and freezing, just place them contents of the bag into a slow cooker, turn it on for a few hours, and then come home to a complete meal. It takes all the fuss out of cooking and is budget- and health-friendly.

In addition, these recipes will give you more variety than you can ever imagine. Every recipe uses fresh ingredients and the perfect blend of spices. The end result is divine.

So with all these benefits, why not get started and enjoy your freezer to table cooking immediately? Let's get busy!

IT'S ALL IN THE PREP!

Although you may be excited about getting started, it is important that you go over the steps of the prep work since this is where you will be putting in the most time. The ease of these meals is simply because you can do a month of meals in one afternoon. However, if you are not properly prepared, it can quickly become a hassle to create them. To prevent that from happening, be sure to read through this chapter.

Steps for Freezing

Step One: Read through the book

Take the time to really go through this book and pick out the meals that you want to try. Also, decide if there are a few that you would like to double up.

Step Two: Compile a shopping list

Next, go over each recipe you want to make and check your cupboards to see what you have. Write down anything that you don't have. One tip for spices -- if yours are over three months old, consider buying new spices. Their freshness will further the best flavor in your dishes.

Step Three: Get all of your supplies

Go shopping for your groceries. Don't forget to pick up several packages of freezer bags in several different sizes. Remember that some meals may require you to use two or more freezer bags.

Step Four: Clean your kitchen

You want as clean of a workspace as possible. This also means cleaning your freezer out to make room for your new meals.

Step Five: Write out special cooking instructions

Go through each recipe, and with a Sharpie pen, write out the special cooking instructions on each bag. This can be the temperature to cook at, when to add special ingredients, and how to serve.

Step Six: Mass produce some items

This is possible only with certain ingredients, such as chopped onions, and I only recommend doing it when you have a actual measurement outside of one onion. If you create bins filled with the common chopped vegetables, you can create an assembly line style for making your meals.

Step Seven: Get prepping

Once you have done all the other steps, you can start prepping your meals. Try to do them in groups according to meats. In other words, you would do all the beef recipes, then all the pork, then all the chicken. Wash knives, counters, bowls, and cutting boards between each recipe.

Step Eight: Label

After each recipe is done, label the bag, attach the instructions card, and seal everything up. Always use clean freezer bags to prevent cross contamination.

Step Nine: Freeze

Finally, freeze the bags as you are finish up each recipe. Put each bag in the freezer as you finish it. Keep your foods chilled as you work. Don't leave the food for future recipes on the counter to get warm as bacteria can start to build.
And that is all there is to getting a month full of meals.

A Word on Safety

When it comes to safety, it's always good to consider several points. Remember that you are working with several different foods when you are prepping, and you can create opportunities where you can contaminate your food if you're not careful. For that reason, it is important to follow some standard safety tips.

1. Always have multiple cutting boards.

When you are cooking, make sure that you have multiple cutting boards. You should have a one designated for meats and a different one for fruits and vegetables. **In addition, always wash your cutting boards between each meal you prepare.** It may seem like a hassle, but it will prevent contamination.

2. Start with a clutter-free kitchen.

Of course you will need clean counter but make sure you clear your kitchen of anything you don't need. Creating a large number of meals at once can fill your kitchen quickly. Keeping your kitchen clutter free helps make sure that you don't accidentally contaminate food or get injured while you work.

3. Work on one recipe at a time.

Although it can be tempting to work on several, you can actually cause a lot of problems with your meals if you do. As I have mentioned, you can risk cross contamination, which can lead to food poisoning. In addition, you can make mistakes more easily with the recipes, which could ruin your meal.

When you are done with the recipe, clean up the area, and put things away before moving on to the next recipe. Also, place your freezer bags into the freezer. The sooner you get them in, the better.

4. Label, label, label.

I can't emphasize the importance of this too much, since labelling will ensure that you never eat rotten food. One thing to stress is that frozen slow cooker meals last for 1 to 3 months in a freezer so it is important to mark the date you made the meal. You can also create "best before" dates on all of your foods.

5. Never use frozen meats.

Finally, never use frozen meats. The reason for this is because freezing a meat, thawing it to use in a recipe, and then refreezing can open the meat up to bacteria.

Some Tips About Freezing

Now that we have those tips, let's look at some other tips for freezing.

Tip Number 1: Always Cool the Food

While it can be tempting, never freeze hot food. Instead, allow it to cool down before you put it in the freezer. There are several reasons for this. One, the food may lose some of its flavor and consistency if it gets the shock of going from hot to freezing too quickly. Two, it will take longer to freeze, which will cost you more in electricity. Three, the hot food could potentially dethaw other food in your freezer, which open up the possibility of food poisoning.

Tip Number 2: Throw Old Food Out

This goes back to the importance of labelling your freezer bags. Unfortunately, sometimes labels can be rubbed off. If you doubt the age of your food, throw it out. This, too, will help lower the possibility of getting food poisoning.

Tip Number 3: Work with Fresh Food

When you are setting up to prep your meals, use fresh food. Starting with fresh food will ensure that you have the best flavor in your meals. Remember that freezing old food that is starting to spoil will not save the dish. It will actually fill the dish with the taste of old food and make the meals unpalatable.

Tip Number 4: Keep the Freezer Stocked

Want to make sure that your freezer is being as economical as your meal planning? Keep it stocked. The more food that is in the freezer, the less air flow there is. This means that the food stays colder because the food is keeping itself cold. Your freezer will not have to work as hard, and it will save you money.

CHICKEN AND TURKEY RECIPES

Rich in flavor and culture, these dishes can bring international delights to your slow cooker. These are easy to make, and they are the perfect slow cooker recipe to freeze. All of these recipes can be stand-alone meals, or you can serve them with your favorite sides.

Lemon Chicken

Servings: 8
Preparation time: 15 minutes
Cooking time: 6 hours

Ingredients:

2 lbs of chicken breast, boneless and skinless
2 garlic cloves
1/2 cup of chicken broth
3 tbsp of lemon juice
1 tsp of dried oregano
1 tsp of dried parsley
1/2 tsp of seasoning salt, msg free
1/4 tsp of ground pepper
2 tbsp of water
Non-stick cooking spray

Directions:

To Prepare for Freezing

- Remove all of the skin and bone of the chicken breast. You can also purchase boneless/skinless chicken breasts. Cut the chicken breasts into eight 4-oz servings.
- In a separate bowl, combine together the oregano, parsley, seasoning salt, and ground pepper. Mix well.
- Rub the seasoning onto the chicken, and place the chicken into a freezer bag.
- In a separate bowl, whisk together the lemon juice and broth.
- Mince the garlic, and add to the broth mixture.
- Whisk until it is well blended.
- Pour into a separate freezer bag and seal.
- Place both the chicken freezer bag and the broth freezer bag into a larger freezer bag.
- Seal and label the larger bag with the name of the dish, the date you prepped the meal, the cooking time, and the heat setting.
- Freeze.

To Slow Cook

- To cook, take out of freezer.
- Using a non-stick cooking spray, coat the slow cooker.
- Arrange the chicken in the bottom of the slow cooker.
- Place the broth on top of the chicken (it can still be a frozen lump).
- Add the 2 tbsp of water.

- Set the slow cooker to low heat, and cook the chicken for 6 to 8 hours.
- Serve on a bed of rice or with your favorite side dishes.

Nutrition facts per serving (135 g)

Calories: 221
Total fat: 8.6 g.
Carbohydrates: 0.6 g.
Dietary fiber: 0 g.
Sugars: 0 g.
Protein: 33.2 g.

Chicken and Dumplings

Servings: 6
Preparation time: 20 minutes
Cooking time: 6 to 8 hours

Ingredients:

6 chicken breasts, boneless and skinless
1 cup of milk
1 cup of water
4 tbsp of butter
1 cup of red onions, diced
1/2 cup of carrots, peeled and shredded
1/2 tsp of ground pepper
1 tsp of rosemary
1 1/2 cups of cream of chicken soup
1 can of prepared Biscuits such as Pillsbury

Directions:

To Prepare for Freezing

- Remove all of the skin and bone of the chicken breast. You can also purchase boneless/skinless chicken breasts. Keep the chicken breasts whole. You will be shredding them near the end of the cooking phase.
- In a small bowl, combine the rosemary and pepper.
- Rub onto the chicken breasts. Place the chicken breasts into a freezer bag. Seal completely.
- Wash and peel the carrots. Shred and place into a bowl.

- Wash, peel and chop the onion. Mix with the carrots.
- Once they are mixed. Spoon half of the mixture into a small bowl, and add 3/4 cup of cream of chicken soup. Mix thoroughly before transferring to a freezer bag. Seal.
- Place the remaining carrots and onions into a separate freezer bag and seal.
- In another freezer bag, add the remaining cream of chicken soup and the butter. Make sure the butter is in chunks.
- Seal.
- Place all three bags into a larger freezer bag. Seal and label the larger bag with the name of the dish, the date you prepped the meal, the cooking time, and the heat setting.
- Freeze.

To Slow Cook

- Take the bags out of the freezer.
- On the bottom, place the carrot-onions, and soup mixture.
- Top with the chicken breasts.
- Cover with the remaining carrots and onion mixture.
- Place the remaining soup and butter mixture on the top of the carrot mixture.
- All of the layers will be hard lumps but don't worry, it will even out with the cooking process.
- Add one cup of water.
- Set the slow cooker to low, and allow cooking for 5 to 7 hours.

- After the set time, use a fork and shred the chicken. You can also take the chicken out and shred it in a blender but by this point, the chicken should be easy to shred with just a fork and knife.
- If you removed the chicken, return it to the slow cooker.
- Add one cup of milk, and stir until it is well blended.
- Remove the biscuits from their container. Place on the top of the mixture in the slow cooker.
- Replace the lid of the slow cooker, and continue cooking for another hour. It is ready when the biscuits are cooked on the inside.
- Serve with noodles, on its own, or with a favorite side dish.

***Nutrition facts per serving* (336 g)**
Calories: 421
Total fat: 22.4 g.
Carbohydrates: 9.4 g.
Dietary fiber: 0.8 g.
Sugars: 3.5 g.
Protein: 43.2 g.

Aloha Chicken

Servings: 8
Preparation time: 20 minutes
Cooking time: 6 hours

Ingredients:

6 chicken breasts, boneless and skinless
6 garlic cloves
1 cup of white vinegar
1 cup of pineapple juice
2 1/2 cups of pineapple, chunks (20 ounce can)
1 cup of sugar, white
4 tbsp of soy sauce

Directions:

To Prepare for Freezing

- Remove all of the skin and bone of the chicken breast. You can also purchase boneless/skinless chicken breasts. Keep the chicken breasts whole. You will be shredding them near the end of the cooking phase.
- Place the chicken into a large freezer bag, but leave it unsealed. Set aside.
- In a large bowl, whisk together the white vinegar, soy sauce, and pineapple juice.
- Add the sugar, and stir until the sugar dissolves.
- Using large chunks, add the pineapple. Don't use crushed pineapple. In addition, it is better to use canned pineapple to avoid hard chunks in your meal.

- Mince the garlic, and add to the pineapple mixture. Whisk until well blended.
- Pour the mixture into the bag containing the chicken.
- Seal and label the freezer bag with name of the dish, the date you prepped the meal, the cooking time, and the heat setting.
- Freeze.

To Slow Cook

- Remove the bag from the freezer, and place the contents into a slow cooker.
- Turn to low, and allow to cook for 5 hours.
- After five hours, shred the chicken and pineapple with a fork and knife. You can also take the chicken and pineapple out and shred it in a blender but by this point, the chicken and pineapple should be easy to shred with just a fork and knife.
- Return the chicken and pineapple to the slow cooker if you removed it. Stir completely.
- Replace lid and continue cooking for an additional hour.
- Serve with rice.

Nutrition facts per serving (201 g)
Calories: 256
Total fat: 3.0 g.
Carbohydrates: 55.2 g.
Dietary fiber: 0.7 g.
Sugars: 26.8 g.
Protein: 2 g.

Teriyaki Chicken

Servings: 8
Preparation time: 15 minutes
Cooking time: 6 hours

Ingredients:

8 chicken thighs, boneless and skinless
1/4 cup of brown sugar
2/3 cup of brown sugar
4 garlic cloves
1 1/2 tsp of fresh ginger
1 tsp of sesame oil
3 tbsp of mirin
3 tsp of cornstarch
1 1/4 cup of water
1 tbsp of honey
1/2 cup of soy sauce
Sliced ginger,

Directions:

To Prepare for Freezing

- In a bowl, whisk together the sesame oil, mirin, and honey.
- Fold in the 1/4 cup of brown sugar.
- Mince 1 garlic clove, and add to the sesame oil mixture.
- Mince the fresh ginger, and fold 1 1/2 teaspoons into the sesame oil mixture.

- In a separate bowl, mix together a 1/4 cup of water and the cornstarch. Add to the sesame oil mixture, and stir until it is well blended. Place in a saucepan, and cook until thickened on low, or roughly 10 minutes.
- Set aside to cool completely.
- Trim the excess fat from the chicken thighs. Keep them whole and set aside.
- In a large bowl, combine the soy sauce, remaining water, and remaining brown sugar. Mix until the brown sugar has dissolved.
- Mince the remaining garlic, and whisk into the soy sauce mixture.
- Make 3 to 5 slices of ginger, and add to the mixture.
- Stir in the teriyaki sauce mixture that you made.
- Add the chicken and toss.
- Pour into a freezer bag and seal.
- Seal and label the freezer bag with the name of the dish, the date you prepped the meal, the cooking time, and the heat setting.
- Freeze.

To Slow Cook

- Run the freezer bag under warm water for about 30 seconds or until you see a small amount of liquid in the bag.
- Pour the contents of the freezer bag into the slow cooker.
- Set temperature to low.
- Cook for 4 to 6 hours.
- Serve warm with egg noodles or rice.

Nutrition facts per serving *(374 g)*

Calories: 601

Total fat: 16.8 g.

Carbohydrates: 47.9 g.

Dietary fiber: 0 g.

Sugars: 40.1 g.

Protein: 63.1 g.

Chicken with Black Bean and Corn Salsa

Servings: 8
Preparation time: 20 minutes
Cooking time: 6 hours

Ingredients:

6 chicken breasts, boneless and skinless
2 cups of corn, canned or frozen
2 cups of black beans
3/4 cup of water
1 cup of salsa
1 tbsp of chili powder
1/4 tsp of onion powder
1/2 tsp of paprika
1/4 tsp of garlic powder
1/4 tsp of oregano flakes
1 1/2 tsp of ground cumin
1/4 tsp of crushed red pepper flakes
1 tsp of salt
1 tsp of black pepper
1 cup of cheddar cheese, shredded

Garnish Ingredients (Do Not Freeze)
1 cup of sour cream
1/2 cup of lettuce, shredded
1 large tomato
1 small avocado
Hot sauce to taste

Directions:

To Prepare for Freezing

- Remove all of the skin and bone of the chicken breast. You can also purchase boneless/skinless chicken breasts. Keep the chicken breasts whole. You will be shredding them near the end of the cooking phase. Set aside.
- Drain and rinse the black beans. Place into a large bowl.
- Drain the corn. Add to the black beans.
- In a small bowl, mix together the spices. This creates a spicy taco seasoning that can be used for more than this recipe. Whisk them together so they are well blended.
- Add to the black bean and corn mixture. Toss until the beans are coated.
- Place the bean mixture into a freezer bag. Seal.
- Place the chicken breasts into a separate freezer bag.
- Pour the salsa into the chicken breast freezer bag.
- Seal.
- Shred the cheddar cheese and place into a small freezer bag.
- Place the 2 bags into a larger freezer bag. Seal and label the larger bag with the date you prepped the meal as well as the cooking time and heat setting.
- Freeze.

To Slow Cook

- Remove food from the freezer.
- Place the bean and corn mixture on the bottom of the slow cooker.
- Add the chicken and lay it on top of the bean mixture.
- Set the slow cooker to low, and cook the chicken for 5 hours.
- Once it is cooked, take a fork and shred the chicken. Stir so the mixture is well blended.
- Cook for another hour before serving warm.
- You can garnish with any or all of the ingredients that are listed as garnishes. Be sure to wash, peel, and cut as necessary. Tomatoes and avocadoes should be diced, and lettuce and cheese should be shredded.
- Serve with corn chips or on rice.

Nutrition facts per serving before garnish (252 g)

Calories: 413
Total fat: 9.2 g.
Carbohydrates: 41.1 g.
Dietary fiber: 9.2 g.
Sugars: 3.4 g.
Protein: 42.7 g.

Chicken Tikka Masala

Servings: 4
Preparation time: 10 minutes
Cooking time: 8 hours

Ingredients:

1 1/2 lbs of chicken, boneless and skinless
1/2 cup of heavy cream
1 medium onion
2 garlic cloves
1 tbsp of lemon juice
2 tbsp of tomato paste
1/2 of an English Cucumber
1 3/4 cups of crushed tomatoes, canned
1 tsp of salt
1 tsp of black pepper
2 tsp of garam masala spice
1/4 cup of cilantro leaves

Directions:

To Prepare for Freezing

- Remove all of the skin and bone of the chicken breast. You can also purchase boneless/skinless chicken breasts. Keep the chicken breasts whole. You will be shredding them near the end of the cooking phase. Set aside.
- In a bowl, whisk together the tomato paste and tomatoes.
- Chop the garlic and add to the tomato mixture.
- Wash, peel, and chop the onion. Toss in the tomato mixture.

- Fold in the pepper and salt and garam masala. Mix until well blended.
- Place the chicken into the sauce, and turn until it is coated.
- Pour into a freezer bag.
- Place all the bags into a larger freezer bag. Seal and label the larger bag name of the dish, the date you prepped the meal, the cooking time, and the heat setting.
- Freeze.

To Slow Cook

- On the morning you are making the dish, take out the cucumber and half it. Using one half, half it again, and create thin slices.
- Shred the fresh cilantro, and place in a bowl. Add the cucumber to the cilantro.

- Pour in the lemon juice.
- Add the salt and pepper and toss.
- Cover and place in the fridge for 4 to 8 hours. Use it before 8 hours or it will go sour.
- Place all of the contents of the freezer bag into the slow cooker.
- Set temperature to low.
- Cook for 7 to 8 hours. You can also cook it on high, but monitor it to prevent burning. If you cook on high, it will be done in 3 to 4 hours.
- After 6 hours, shred the chicken with a fork. Stir and then cook it for an additional hour.
- Right before it is finished, fold the cream into the mixture. Blend thoroughly.

Serve warm with rice and garnish with the cucumber mixture.

Nutrition facts per serving (355g)
Calories: 388
Total fat: 11.3 g.
Saturated Fat: 5.0 g.
Carbohydrates: 17.2 g.
Dietary fiber: 6.1 g.
Sugars: 8.4 g.
Protein: 54.0 g.

Provençale Chicken Supper

Servings: 6
Preparation time: 10 minutes
Cooking time: 7 hours

Ingredients:

1 1/2 lbs of chicken breast, boneless and skinless
2 cups of cannellini beans (16 oz can)
1 yellow bell pepper
1 red bell pepper
1 tbsp of dried thyme
2 tbsp of dried basil
1 3/4 cups of diced tomatoes with basil and oregano (1-14.5oz can)

Directions:

To Prepare for Freezing

- Wash, seed, and chop the red and yellow bell peppers.
- Drain the beans, and wash them.
- Place the beans and peppers into a freezer bag, and shake so they are well blended. Seal the bag, and set to the side.
- Remove the skin and bone from the breast if you did not purchase it skinless and boneless.
- In a small bowl, whisk together the basil and thyme.
- Add the diced tomatoes, and stir until it is well blended.
- Place the chicken in a freezer bag.

- Pour the tomato mixture into the bag. Seal completely.
- Place both the chicken freezer bag and the veggie freezer bag into a larger freezer bag.
- Seal and label the larger bag with the date you prepped the meal as well as the cooking time and heat setting.
- Freeze.

To Slow Cook

- To cook, take out of freezer.
- Remove the chicken bag and run it, sealed, under water for 1 to 2 minutes or until you have a small amount of liquid in the bag.
- Open and pour the chicken mixture into the slow cooker.
- Set the slow cooker to low heat.
- Add the vegetables and beans to the slow cooker on top of the chicken.
- Cover and cook for 7 hours or until the chicken is fully cooked.
- Serve warm.

Nutrition facts per serving (236g)
Calories: 366
Calories from Fat: 45
Total fat: 4.7 g.
Carbohydrates: 40.7 g.
Dietary fiber: 16.6 g.
Sugars: 3.5 g.
Protein: 40.4 g.

Chicken with Potatoes and Carrots

Servings: 6
Preparation time: 10 minutes
Cooking time: 3 hours and 30 minutes

Ingredients:

6 bone-in chicken thighs, skinless
2 cups of baby carrots
6 red potatoes
1 tbsp of thyme
3/4 tsp of salt
1/2 tsp of pepper
1 tsp of paprika
1 garlic clove
1/2 cup of chicken broth
1 tsp of olive oil
1 3/4 cups of sliced onion
1/2 cup of dry white wine

Directions:

To Prepare for Freezing

- Wash, peel, and slice the onion. Place in a bowl.
- Wash the baby carrots, and add to the onion.
- Wash and chop the potatoes into bite-sized pieces. Add to the onions, and mix.
- In a separate bowl, whisk together the 1/2 teaspoon of salt and 1/4 teaspoon of pepper.
- Pour in the broth, and mix well.
- Mince garlic, and add to the broth.

- Add the white wine and the thyme. Mix until it is well blended.
- Pour the broth mixture over the vegetables, and mix well.
- Transfer to a freezer bag, and seal.
- Remove the skin from your chicken thighs.
- In a small bowl, combine the remaining salt and pepper with the paprika. Mix well.
- Rub the paprika mixture onto the chicken thighs.
- Place the chicken into a freezer bag, and seal.
- Place both the chicken freezer bag and the broth freezer bag into a larger freezer bag.
- Seal and label the larger bag with the date you prepped the meal as well as the cooking time and heat setting.
- Freeze.

To Slow Cook

- To cook, take out of freezer.
- Add the oil to the slow cooker, and set it to low.
- Place the chicken in the slow cooker.
- Run the broth under the tap for a few minutes until you see a small amount of juice in the bag. Empty into the slow cooker over the chicken.
- Cover and cook for 3 1/2 hours or until the chicken is cooked and the vegetables are tender.
- Serve warm.

Nutrition facts per serving (377g)
Calories: 295
Calories from Fat: 39
Total fat: 4.3 g.
Carbohydrates: 38.8 g.
Dietary fiber: 4.8 g.
Sugars: 4.1 g.
Protein: 20.9 g.

Chicken Korma

Servings: 6
Preparation time: 10 minutes
Cooking time: 6 hours and 15 minutes

Ingredients:

2 lbs of chicken breast, boneless and skinless
1 cinnamon stick
2 bay leaves
4 garlic cloves
2 tbsp of minced ginger
1 onion
2 tsp of curry powder
1 tsp of coriander, ground
1/2 tsp of red pepper
1/2 tsp of cumin, ground
1 tsp of salt
1/4 cup of fresh cilantro
1/2 cup of plain yogurt
1 3/4 cup of diced tomatoes (14.5oz can)
2 cups of baking potatoes

Directions:

To Prepare for Freezing

- Remove the skin and bone from the chicken breast if you did not purchase it skinless and boneless.
- Chop into bite-sized pieces.
- Wash, peel, and chop the onion. Toss with the chicken cubes.

- Mince the ginger, and add it to the chicken mixture.
- Add the red pepper flakes, coriander, curry, and cumin. Mix well.
- Mince the garlic and add. Mix well.
- Place the chicken mixture into a freezer bag, and seal.
- Drain the tomatoes, and add to a bowl.
- Whisk in the salt.
- Wash and chop the potatoes. Add to the tomatoes, and mix well.
- Pour into a separate freezer bag and seal.
- Place both the chicken freezer bag and the potato freezer bag into a larger freezer bag.
- Seal and label the larger bag with the date you prepped the meal as well as the cooking time and heat setting.
- Freeze.

To Slow Cook

- To cook, take out of freezer.
- Pour the ingredients from both bags into a slow cooker.
- Set the slow cooker to low.
- Add in the cinnamon stick and the bay leaves.
- Cook for 6 hours or until the potatoes are tender and the chicken is cooked.
- After it is cooked, turn off the slow cooker, and allow the chicken mixture to stand for 15 minutes.
- When the time has passed, add the yogurt, and mix well.
- Serve warm with your favorite noodle or rice.

Nutrition facts per serving (406g)
Calories: 367
Calories from Fat: 56
Total fat: 6.2 g.
Carbohydrates: 25.6 g.
Dietary fiber: 3.6 g.
Sugars: 4.2 g.
Protein: 52.7 g.

Mediterranean Chicken

Servings: 6
Preparation time: 15 minutes
Cooking time: 7 hours

Ingredients:

12 chicken thighs, bone in, skinned
1 3/4 cups of onions, chopped
2 tbsp of drained capers
1 3/4 cups of whole plum tomatoes (1-14.5oz can)
1/4 cup of pitted kalamata olives
1 tbsp of olive oil
1/4 tsp of black pepper
1 lemon

Directions:

To Prepare for Freezing

- Remove the skin from the chicken thighs. Set to the side.
- Take the lemon, and remove the rind. You want to have 1 teaspoon of grated rind. Place in a small bag, and seal.
- Squeeze the lemon, and reserve 1 tablespoon of lemon juice. Place in a medium-sized bowl.
- Wash, peel, and chop the onions. Add to the lemon juice.
- Cut the olives in half, and add to the onions.
- Drain the capers, and mix into the ingredients.
- Take the plum tomatoes, and coarsely chop them. Drain the excess liquid.

- Add the tomatoes to the lemon juice mixture, and stir until it is well blended.
- Pour the tomato mixture into a freezer bag, and seal.
- Rub the pepper onto the chicken. Place in a separate freezer bag, and seal.
- Place both the chicken freezer bag, lemon rind bag, and the tomato mixture freezer bag into a larger freezer bag.
- Seal and label the larger bag with the date you prepped the meal as well as the cooking time and heat setting.
- Freeze.

To Slow Cook

- To cook, take out of freezer.
- Add the oil to the slow cooker.
- Turn on the slow cooker, and set the temperature to low.
- Place the chicken on the bottom of the slow cooker.
- Place the tomato mixture on top.
- Cover and cook for 4 hours until the chicken is fully cooked.
- Remove the chicken, and set aside.
- Add the lemon rind to the sauce in the slow cooker. Mix well.
- To serve, pour the sauce over the chicken.

Nutrition facts per serving (355g)

Calories: 591
Calories from Fat: 213
Total fat: 23.7 g.
Carbohydrates: 6.6 g.
Dietary fiber: 2.2 g.
Sugars: 3.2 g.
Protein: 81.9 g.

Chicken Enchiladas

Servings: 6
Preparation time: 15 minutes
Cooking time: 8 hours

Ingredients:

4 chicken breasts, boneless and skinless (about 1 1/2 lbs)
2 cups of chicken broth
1 tsp of salt
2 tsp of cumin, ground
1/3 cup of chili powder
1 tsp of oregano
1 tsp of salt
1 garlic clove
1/8 tsp of cayenne pepper
1/2 cup of flour, all purpose
1 3/4 cup of diced tomatoes (1-14oz can)
6 Tortilla shells

Directions:

To Prepare for Freezing

- In a blender, mix together the chili powder and chicken broth.
- Peel the garlic clove, and add it to the ingredients.
- Fold in the flour, cumin, and salt.
- Add the oregano and cayenne pepper.
- Mix the ingredients until they are smooth.
- Remove the skin and bone from the chicken breast if you did not purchase it skinless and boneless.

- Place the chicken into a large freezer bag.
- Pour the chicken broth mixture into the same bag.
- Seal and label the larger bag with the date you prepped the meal as well as the cooking time and heat setting.

To Slow Cook

To cook, take out of freezer, and place in the slow cooker.

Set the temperature to low, and cook for 8 hours.

A half hour before it is done, take two forks, and shred the chicken by inserting the forks into the chicken and pulling it apart.

Stir well, and finish cooking.

Serve warm on tortilla shells with your favorite toppings.

Nutrition facts per serving (338g)
Calories: 748
Calories from Fat: 323
Total fat: 35.9 g.
Carbohydrates: 64.4 g.
Dietary fiber: 6.4 g.
Sugars: 2.9 g.
Protein: 39.1 g.

Sweet and Spicy Satsuma Turkey

Servings: 6
Preparation time: 20 minutes
Cooking time: 4 hours and 15 minutes

Ingredients:

3 3/4 lbs of turkey thighs, bone in and skinned
3 cups of red onion, sliced
2/3 cup of orange juice
2 tsp of five spice powder
1 tsp of salt
1/2 tsp of crushed red pepper
2 tsp of tamarind paste
3/4 cup of Riesling
2 cups of Satsuma mandarin orange sections (7 oranges)
1 1/2 tbsp of cornstarch
1 tbsp of canola oil
1/3 cup of orange marmalade

Directions:

To Prepare for Freezing

- In a large bowl, whisk together the orange juice and the orange marmalade.
- Add in the tamarind paste.
- Stir in the crushed red pepper.
- Fold in the Riesling, and mix well.
- Wash, peel, and thinly slice the onion. Add to the orange juice mixture.
- Pour the ingredients into a freezer bag, and seal.

- In a small bowl, whisk together the salt and the five spice powders.
- Rub the spice onto the turkey legs.
- Place the turkey legs into a freezer bag. Seal.
- Place both the turkey freezer bag and the orange juice mixture freezer bag into a larger freezer bag.
- Seal and label the larger bag with the date you prepped the meal as well as the cooking time and heat setting.
- Freeze.

To Slow Cook

- To cook, take out of freezer.
- Add the oil to the slow cooker.
- Turn on the slow cooker, and set the temperature to medium.
- Place the turkey legs on the bottom of the slow cooker.
- Add the orange juice mixture on top of the turkey.
- Peel, and separate the sections of the oranges. Add them to the slow cooker.
- Cook for 4 hours or until the turkey is cooked through.
- Carefully remove the turkey from the slow cooker. Remove the bones, and throw them away, reserving the meat on a platter.
- Pour the sauce that is in the slow cooker into a medium sauce pan.
- Place the saucepan on the stove, and set the temperature to medium high.
- Remove 1/4 cup of the liquid, and mix the cornstarch into the 1/4 cup of liquid.

- Pour the cornstarch mixture back into the saucepan, and stir until it is completely incorporated.
- Bring to a boil, and continue cooking until the sauce has thickened, about 1 to 2 minutes.
- Remove from heat, and cover the turkey with the sauce.
- Serve warm with rice or noodles.

Nutrition facts per serving (252g)
Calories: 286
Calories from Fat: 76
Total fat: 8.4 g.
Carbohydrates: 40.6 g.
Dietary fiber: 2.5 g.
Sugars: 28.1 g.
Protein: 9.7 g.

Sesame-Ginger Chicken

Servings: 6
Preparation time: 10 minutes
Cooking time: 30 minutes

Ingredients:

3-4 lb whole chicken
2 tsp of rice wine vinegar
1/2 cup of water
2 tbsp of sesame seeds
1 tbsp of fresh ginger, minced
1/4 cup of honey
2 tbsp of dark sesame oil
1/2 tsp of red pepper flakes
1/2 cup of soy sauce
3 garlic cloves

Directions:

To Prepare for Freezing

- Rinse the chicken, and pat dry with a paper towel.
- Using a sharp knife, cut the chicken into pieces. You want two legs, two breasts, and two wings. Throw away the back and as much skin as possible. Set aside.
- In a large bowl, whisk together the honey and wine vinegar.
- Add the water.
- Stir in the sesame seeds and the sesame oil.
- Mince the garlic and ginger, and add to the mixture.
- Fold in the red pepper flakes.

- Add the soy sauce, and mix well.
- Place the chicken into the freezer bag, and pour the sesame seed mixture into the bag.
- Seal and label with the date you prepped the meal as well as the cooking time and heat setting.
- Freeze.

To Slow Cook

- To cook, take out of freezer.
- Run the bag under the hot water for about 2 minutes until you see juice starting to form in the bag.
- Empty the contents into the slow cooker.
- Set the temperature to low, and cook the chicken for 8 hours or until the chicken is cooked.
- When it is done, carefully remove the chicken. Remove the bones and any extra skin that was left on.
- Serve the chicken with rice or noodles.

Nutrition facts per serving (160g)
Calories: 259
Calories from Fat: 81
Total fat: 8.9 g.
Carbohydrates: 15.2 g.
Dietary fiber: 0.7 g.
Sugars: 12.0 g.
Protein: 29.1 g.

Chicken and Shrimp Jambalaya

Servings: 6
Preparation time: 20 minutes
Cooking time: 8 hours

Ingredients:

1 lb of chicken breasts, boneless, skinless
1 onion
1 green pepper
1 lb of andouille sausage
1 lb of cooked shrimp, tailless
1 cup of celery, chopped
2 tsp of Cajun seasoning
1/2 tsp of dried thyme
2 tsp of dried oregano
1 tsp of cayenne pepper
2 tsp of dried parsley
1 cup of chicken broth
3 1/2 cups of diced tomatoes (1-28oz can)

Directions:

To Prepare for Freezing

- Wash and seed the green pepper. Chop it into small, bite-sized pieces.
- Wash and chop the celery.
- Slice the sausage, and place in a bowl with the pepper and celery.
- Wash, peel, and chop the onion. Add to the sausage mixture.

- Remove the skin and bone from the chicken breast if you did not purchase it skinless and boneless. Cut into 1/2 to 1 inch cubes.
- Pour in the chicken broth, and mix well.
- Add the diced tomatoes, and the juice of the diced tomatoes.
- Stir in the Cajun seasoning, thyme, oregano, and parsley.
- Mix well, and transfer to a large freezer bag. Seal
- Place the shrimp in a separate freezer bag, and seal.
- Place both the chicken freezer bag, and the shrimp freezer bag into a larger freezer bag.
- Seal and label the larger bag with the date you prepped the meal as well as the cooking time and heat setting.
- Freeze.

To Slow Cook

- To cook, take out of freezer.
- Pour the entire contents of the chicken freezer bag into the slow cooker.
- Set the slow cooker to low, and cook for 7 1/2 hours or until the chicken is cooked and the spices are dispersed throughout the dish.
- Stir in the shrimp, and continue cooking for an additional 30 minutes.
- Serve warm.

Nutrition facts per serving (411g)

Calories: 533
Calories from Fat: 253
Total fat: 28.1 g.
Carbohydrates: 11.6 g.
Dietary fiber: 2.5 g.
Sugars: 4.6 g.
Protein: 55.7 g.

BEEF RECIPES

For many people, beef meals are on the top of the list when it comes to cooking, and these meals will definitely be on the top of your freezer-to-table choices. They are full of flavor. and take a commonly used meat to new heights.

Western Beef Casserole

Servings: 4
Preparation time: 20 minutes
Cooking time: 4 hours

Ingredients:

1 1/2 pounds of ground beef, lean
1 cup of Spanish onion, chopped
2 cups of corn, canned or frozen
2 cups of kidney beans
1/2 tsp of chili powder
1 1/2 cups of tomato soup
1/4 cup of milk
1 cup of cheddar cheese, grated

Directions:

To Prepare for Freezing

- In a frying pan, cook the ground beef until it is brown.
- Drain excess grease. Place the meat into a large bowl.
- Wash and chop the onion. Add to the ground beef.
- Drain the corn and add to the ground beef. Toss until the ingredients are well blended.
- Drain and wash the kidney beans. Add to the ground beef and mix. Again, you want the ingredients to be well blended to prevent clumps of beans.
- In a separate bowl, whisk together the tomato soup and milk.
- Fold in the chili powder and mix with the tomato soup.
- Pour the soup mixture over the ground beef mixture. Mix.
- Once it is mixed, carefully spoon the mixture into a large freezer bag. Seal.
- Shred the cheddar cheese, and place into a small freezer bag.
- Place the meat freezer bag and the cheese freezer bag into a larger freezer bag.
- Seal and label the freezer bag with name of the dish, the date you prepped the meal, the cooking time, and the heat setting.
- Freeze.

To Slow Cook

- Remove the ingredients from the freezer.
- Place the cheese in the fridge to use later.
- Pour the meat mixture into the slow cooker.
- Set the slow cooker to low and cook for 3 hours.
- After 3 hours, remove the cheese from the freezer bag and sprinkle on the top of the ground beef mixture.
- Stir until the cheese is dispersed evenly throughout the mixture.
- Replace lid and continue cooking for 1 hour.
- Serve warm with a nice biscuit.

Nutrition facts per serving (506 g)
Calories: 879
Total fat: 22.3 g.
Carbohydrates: 87.9 g.
Dietary fiber: 17.6 g.
Sugars: 14 g.
Protein: 83.6 g.

Sweet and Sour Beef

Servings: 6
Preparation time: 15 minutes
Cooking time: 7 to 8 hours

Ingredients:

2 1/2 lbs of stewing beef (or a chuck steak or roast as an alternative)
1/2 cup of beef broth
2 tbsp of soy sauce
5 tbsp of red wine vinegar
1/2 cup of pineapple juice
2 garlic cloves
2 large cooking onions
1 red bell pepper
1 green bell pepper
2 large tomatoes
2 1/2 cups of pineapple, chunked and unsweetened
3 tbsp of brown sugar
3/4 tsp of seasoned salt, msg free
1/4 tsp of pepper
3/4 tsp of paprika
1 1/2 tbsp of cornstarch

Directions:

To Prepare for Freezing

- In a large bowl, add the pineapple juice.
- Wash and peel the onions. Cut into wedges. Add to the pineapple juice.
- Add in all of the spices.
- Pour in the beef broth.

- Finally, add 3 tbsp of the red wine vinegar. Whisk until it is well blended.
- Cut the stewing beef into bite sized cubes. Place in the pineapple juice mixture.
- Stir until the meat is coated.
- Pour into a freezer bag and seal.
- Wash and seed the red and green bell peppers.
- Place in a bowl and toss with the brown sugar.
- Spoon into a second freezer bag and seal.
- In a small bowl, mix together the corn starch, soy sauce, and red wine vinegar. Place into a small freezer bag.
- Wash and cut the tomatoes into wedges.
- Add to the pineapple chunks in a bowl and mix.
- Transfer to a separate freezer bag.
- Place all of the ingredient bags into a large freezer bag.
- Seal and label the freezer bag with name of the dish, the date you prepped the meal, the cooking time, and the heat setting.
- Freeze.

To Slow Cook

- Remove the ingredients from the freezer.
- Place the pepper bag, tomato bag, and the cornstarch bag into the fridge to use later.
- Place the stewing beef mixture into the slow cooker.
- Set the slow cooker to low and allow the meat to cook for 6 to 6 ½ hours.
- Turn the temperature to high on the slow cooker.
- Fold in the green pepper mixture and the cornstarch mixture.

- Mix until it is well blended.
- Replace cover and cook for an additional hour.
- About 15 minutes before serving, stir in the tomato and pineapple mixture.
- Serve warm with rice, noodles or a favorite side dish.

Nutrition facts per serving (475g)
Calories: 477
Total fat: 12.3 g.
Carbohydrates: 28.5 g.
Dietary fiber: 3.9 g.
Sugars: 18.8 g.
Protein: 59.9 g.

Crockpot Meatloaf

Servings: 6
Preparation time: 15 minutes
Cooking time: 6 hours

Ingredients:

1 1/2 lbs of ground beef, lean
3/4 cup of breadcrumbs
1/2 cup of milk
1 packages of dry onion soup mix
2 eggs
1 cups of ketchup
1 tsp of Worcestershire sauce
1/2 cup of brown sugar
1/4 tsp of ginger, ground
1/4 tsp of black pepper
1 tsp of salt
Non-stick cooking spray

Directions:

To Prepare for Freezing

- In a large bowl, mix together the ground beef, breadcrumbs, and onion soup mix.
- Add in the salt and pepper.
- Fold in the ginger.
- Slowly pour in the milk, mixing the ground beef mixture as you do.
- Finally, add the eggs and mix thoroughly.
- Form the ground beef into a loaf, and place into a large freezer bag. *(Optional: you can flatten the ground beef before freezing to save room. When*

you are ready to cook it, thaw completely and form into a loaf before cooking.) Seal.

- In a small bowl, stir together the ketchup and Worcestershire sauce.
- Fold in the brown sugar, and mix until the sugar is dissolved. Pour into a small freezer bag and seal.
- Place all of the ingredient bags into a large freezer bag.
- Seal and label the freezer bag with the name of the dish, the date you prepped the meal, the cooking time, and the heat setting.
- Freeze.

To Slow Cook

- Line the slow cooker with tinfoil.
- Spray with non-stick cooking spray.
- Remove the meatloaf from the freezer, and place in the center of the slow cooker on the tinfoil.
- Place the ketchup bag into the fridge so it can thaw by the end of the day.
- Cook on low for 6 hours.
- Once it is cooked, remove the ketchup packet, and spread the ketchup onto the meatloaf.
- Serve warm with potatoes or other side dishes.
- Cook for an additional 15 to 20 minutes, and then remove by carefully lifting the tinfoil out of the slow cooker.

Nutrition facts per serving *(264 g)*

Calories: 470
Total fat: 11.6 g.
Carbohydrates: 42.8 g.
Dietary fiber: 1.3 g.
Sugars: 27.6 g.
Protein: 47.5 g.

Chinese Beef and Broccoli

Servings: 6
Preparation time: 10 minutes
Cooking time: 8 hours

Ingredients:

2 pounds of stewing beef (or a chuck steak or roast as
an alternative)
2 cups of broccoli florets
1 garlic clove
2 tbsp of cornstarch
1 tbsp of fresh ginger
1/4 cup of soy sauce
1 cup of water
3 tbsp of brown sugar, firmly packed
Non-stick cooking spray

Directions:

To Prepare for Freezing

- Cut the stewing beef into bite-sized pieces. Set aside.
- Chop the garlic and ginger into small pieces. Place into a large bowl together.
- Add the brown sugar and toss.
- Stir in 3/4 cup of water and the soy sauce. Mix until the brown sugar is dissolved.
- Place the stewing beef into the mixture, and turn until the beef is coated.
- Spoon into a large freezer bag.
- Wash and chop the broccoli.
- Place into a separate freezer bag and seal.

- Put the ingredients bag into a larger freezer bag.
- Seal and label the freezer bag with name of the dish, the date you prepped the meal, the cooking time, and the heat setting.
- Freeze.

To Slow Cook
- Spray the slow cooker with the non-stick cooking spray. Be sure to spray the sides as well as the bottom.
- Empty the stewing beef bag into the slow cooker. Place the broccoli bag into the fridge.
- Set to the slow cooker to low, and allow the beef to cook for 7½ hours.
- After the set time, take the cornstarch and combine it with a 1/4 cup of water in a small bowl.
- Whisk until the cornstarch has dissolved.
- Increase the temperature on the slow cooker to high.
- Pour the cornstarch into the slow cooker, and stir until it is completely mixed.
- On the stove, cook the broccoli until it is tender.
- Drain.
- Fold into the beef mixture and continue cooking for 15 minutes.
- Serve warm with egg noodles or rice.

Nutrition facts per serving (239g)
Calories: 328
Total fat: 9.6 g.
Carbohydrates: 10.4 g.
Dietary fiber: 1.0 g.
Sugars: 5.1 g.
Protein: 47.5 g.

Italian Beef Sandwiches

Servings: 10
Preparation time: 15 minutes
Cooking time: 12 hours

Ingredients:

1 rump roast, roughly 5 pounds
1 tsp of garlic powder
1 bay leaf
1 tsp of dried parsley
1 tsp of dried oregano
1 tsp of black pepper
1 tsp of salt
1 tsp of onion powder
3 cups of water
1 package of Italian-style salad dressing mix
(Optional: Italian salad dressing mix can be made with
1 1/2 tsp of garlic powder
1 tbsp of dried parsley
1 tsp of black pepper
1 tsp of ground basil
2 tbsp of salt
1 tsp of white sugar
1 tbsp of onion powder
2 tbsp of dried oregano
1/4 tsp of thyme
1/2 tsp of celery flakes)
10 Italian buns for the sandwich

Directions:

To Prepare for Freezing

- If you are making the salad dressing mix yourself, combine all of the spices in the optional ingredients together. Whisk and store in an airtight container.
- Place 4 teaspoons of your homemade salad dressing mix, or one package of the store-bought salad dressing mix into a saucepan,.
- Add the salt, oregano, onion powder, garlic powder, basil, black pepper, and bay leaf to the saucepan.
- Whisk in the water.
- Place on the stove, and set the temperature to medium low.
- Bring to a boil, stirring frequently.
- Once it is boiling, remove from the heat, and allow to cool completely.
- Trim the fat off of the rump roast, and place the whole roast into a freezer bag.
- Pour in the cooled spice mixture.
- Seal and label the freezer bag with name of the dish, the date you prepped the meal, the cooking time, and the heat setting.
- Freeze.

To Slow Cook

- Remove the bag from the freezer, and run under hot water for 30 seconds until you see a small amount of liquid forming.

- Place the roast into the slow cooker, and pour in the frozen liquid.
- Set the slow cooker to low and cook for 10 to 11 hours. You can speed up cooking by setting the slow cooker to high and cooking for 4 to 5 hours. If it is on high, check it frequently to prevent burning your mixture.
- Once cooked, remove the bay leaf.
- Take two forks and pull apart the roast, shredding it.
- Continue cooking for another hour.
- Serve warm on an Italian sandwich bun with your favorite sides.

Nutrition facts per serving *(305 g)*
Calories: 422
Total fat: 13.9 g.
Carbohydrates: 3.3 g.
Dietary fiber: 0 g.
Sugars: 0 g.
Protein: 70.8 g.

Beef and Mushroom Dinner

Servings: 8
Preparation time: 15 minutes
Cooking time: 10 hours

Ingredients:

3 lbs of stewing beef (or a chuck steak or roast as an alternative)
1 cup of sliced mushrooms
1 package of dry onion soup mix
1/2 cup of apple juice
1 1/2 cups of cream of mushroom soup

Directions:
To Prepare for Freezing

- Slice the stewing beef into bite-sized portions. Set aside.
- Wash the mushrooms and slice them.
- Toss the beef and mushrooms together.
- In a small bowl, combine the mushroom soup and apple juice.
- Mix until it is well blended.
- Fold in the onion soup mix. Mix thoroughly.
- Pour the mushroom soup mix over the beef and mushrooms.
- Mix until the beef is coated.
- Spoon the mixture into a freezer bag.
- Seal and label the freezer bag with the name of the dish, the date you prepped the meal, the cooking time, and the heat setting.
- Freeze.

To Slow Cook

- About 24 hours before you cook this meal, remove it from the freezer and thaw in the fridge.
- When it is thawed, pour the contents of the freezer bag into a slow cooker.
- Set the slow cooker to low, and cook for 10 hours. You can cook it on high, however, but be sure to stir it frequently to keep it from burning. If you cook on high, cook for 6 hours.
- Serve warm with rice or noodles.

Nutrition facts per serving (245g)
Calories: 359
Total fat: 12.0 g.
Carbohydrates: 6.8 g.
Dietary fiber: 0 g.
Sugars: 2.4 g.
Protein: 52.6 g.

PORK RECIPES

Many people don't think of pork as a slow cooker meal, outside of a few pork and beans recipes, but there is a lot that you can do with pork. Here are some amazing recipes that you will reach for time and time again.

Crockpot Ribs

Servings: 4
Preparation time: 20 minutes
Cooking time: 6 hours

Ingredients:

2 full racks of baby ribs, pork, about 5 pounds, cut in half
1 cup of white vinegar
3 cup of ketchup
1 tsp of liquid smoke
1 cup of brown sugar
3 tbsp of seasoned salt

Directions:

To Prepare for Freezing

- Rub the seasoned salt onto the ribs. Set aside.
- In a bowl, whisk together the white vinegar and liquid smoke.
- Add in the brown sugar and mix until the sugar dissolves.
- Fold in the ketchup.
- Pour into a large freezer bag.

- Add the ribs to the freezer bag with the vinegar mixture.
- Seal and label the freezer bag with the name of the dish, the date you prepped the meal, the cooking time, and the heat setting.
- Freeze.

To Slow Cook

- Before you cook the ribs, it is important to thaw the ribs for about 24 hours.
- Once thawed, place the ribs into the slow cooker.
- Pour the liquid over the ribs.
- Set the slow cooker to low, and cook for 6 to 7 hours. *(Optional: You can cook on high but check the ribs frequently to ensure they do not burn. Cook for 3 to 4 hours if cooking on high.)*
- Serve with your favorite sides.

Nutrition facts per serving (342 g)
Calories: 513
Total fat: 20.6 g.
Carbohydrates: 34.8 g.
Dietary fiber: 0 g.
Sugars: 30.6 g.
Protein: 42.1 g.

Sausage with Onions and Peppers

Servings: 6
Preparation time: 20 minutes
Cooking time: 8 hours

Ingredients:

1 1/2 lbs of hot Italian sausage (6 to 8 sausages)
1 yellow onion
2 green bell peppers
3/4 cup of tomato paste
2 cups of tomato sauce

Directions:

To Prepare for Freezing

- Slice the Italian sausages into 1/2 inch slices.
- Place into a frying pan, and fry until the sausage is completely cooked.
- Drain and allow to cool completely.
- Wash and peel onion. Chop into fine pieces.
- Wash, seed, and chop the green peppers.
- Place the onions and green peppers into a bowl.
- Pour in the tomato paste and the tomato sauce.
- Mix thoroughly.
- Toss in the cooled sausages.
- Pour the ingredients into a large freezer bag.
- Seal and label the freezer bag with the name of the dish, the date you prepped the meal, the cooking time, and the heat setting.
- Freeze.

To Slow Cook

- Remove the package from the freezer, and place into a slow cooker.
- Set the temperature to low, and cook for 6 to 8 hours.
- Serve with noodles or on a bun as a sandwich.

Nutrition facts per serving (286g)

Calories: 451
Total fat: 32.6g.
Carbohydrates: 14.7 g.
Dietary fiber: 3.8 g.
Sugars: 9.9 g.
Protein: 25.0 g.

Slow cooker Pineapple Glazed Ham

Servings: 10
Preparation time: 10 minutes
Cooking time: 8 hours

Ingredients:

7 to 8 lb ham, bone in is best
2 cups of brown sugar
2 tbsp of mustard
2 1/2 cups of pineapple chunks (20 oz can)
1/2 cup of pineapple juice

Directions:

To Prepare for Freezing

- In a small bowl, combine the brown sugar with the mustard.
- Mix until you have a paste. You may have to add a bit more mustard to create a nice paste.
- Spread the paste over the ham.
- Place the ham in a freezer bag and seal.
- In a separate freezer bag, pour in the pineapple chunks and pineapple juice. Seal.
- Place both bags into a larger freezer bag. Seal and label the freezer bag with the name of the dish, the date you prepped the meal, the cooking time, and the heat setting.
- Freeze.

To Slow Cook

- Remove the ingredients from the freezer.
- Place the ham in the slow cooker.
- Run the pineapple bag under the water for 30 seconds or until you have some liquid.
- Pour into the slow cooker over the ham.
- Set the slow cooker to low, and cook for 6 to 8 hours.
- Serve warm with your favorite sides.

Nutrition facts per serving (403 g)

Calories: 665
Total fat: 28.0 g.
Carbohydrates: 48.4 g.
Dietary fiber: 5.1 g.
Sugars: 33.6 g.
Protein: 53.6 g.

Creamy Ranch Pork Chops and Potatoes

Servings: 6
Preparation time: 20 minutes
Cooking time: 7 hours

Ingredients:

1 1/2 lbs of pork chops, boneless (6- 4oz pork chops)
2 1/2 cups of cream of chicken soup (2- 10oz cans)
1 cup of milk
6 to 8 medium Russet potatoes
2 packages of dry Ranch dressing mix
(Optional: You can make your own Ranch Dressing Mix.
2 tbsp of dried parsley
2 tsp of garlic powder
2 tsp of dried onion flakes
1 tsp of salt
1 1/2 tsp of dried dill weed
1 tsp of pepper
2 tsp of onion powder
1/3 cup of dry buttermilk)

Directions:

To Prepare for Freezing

- If you are making your own Ranch salad dressing mix, combine all of the ingredients in the optional ingredients list. Store in an airtight container. You will use 4 tablespoons of your Ranch salad dressing mix or two packets of store bought.
- In a bowl, blend together the soup and ranch dressing mix.

- Whisk in the milk, and stir until the ingredients are well blended.
- Pour the mixture into a small freezer bag. Seal.
- Wash the potatoes and chop into bite sized pieces. Leave the skin of the potato on.
- Place the potatoes into a separate freezer bag. Seal.
- Place the whole pork chops into a freezer bag. Seal.
- Put all of the freezer bags into a larger freezer bag. Seal and label the freezer bag with the name of the dish, the date you prepped the meal, the cooking time, and the heat setting.
- Freeze.

To Slow Cook

- Remove from the freezer 24 hours before making, and allow to thaw in the fridge.
- When it is thawed, empty all of the ingredient bags into the slow cooker.
- Stir until the potatoes and pork chops are coated.
- Set temperature to low.
- Cook for 6 to 7 hours.
- Serve warm with a vegetable.

Nutrition facts per serving (492 g)
Calories: 630
Total fat: 35.6 g.
Carbohydrates: 0.6 g.
Dietary fiber: 5.2 g.
Sugars: 5.4 g.
Protein: 33.1 g.

Pulled Pork

Servings: 8
Preparation time: 15 minutes
Cooking time: 8 hours

Ingredients:

4 lbs pork roast, boneless (shoulder is best)
1 yellow onion
1/4 cup of red wine vinegar
1/2 cup of honey
3 tbsp of olive oil
3 tbsp of paprika
2 tsp of black pepper
2 tbsp of salt
1/2 tsp of dried thyme
1 tsp of cayenne pepper
1 tsp of garlic powder

Directions:

To Prepare for Freezing

- In a bowl, combine the pepper, garlic powder, salt, and thyme. Whisk together.
- Whisk in the paprika and cayenne pepper.
- In a separate bowl, whisk together the olive oil, vinegar, and honey.
- Pour into the spice mixture, and blend until you have a nice paste.
- Cut the pork roast in half.
- Spread the paste over both halves of the pork roast.
- Place into a freezer bag.

- Wash, peel, and chop the onion.
- Put in the freezer bag with the roast.
- Seal and label the freezer bag with the name of the dish, the date you prepped the meal, the cooking time, and the heat setting.
- Freeze.

To Slow Cook

- When you are ready to use, remove from freezer.
- Place the roast into the slow cooker.
- Close the freezer bag and run it under water to warm up any of the paste that has stuck to the bag.
- Pour any paste that is left in the bag over the pork roasts.
- Set the slow cooker to low.
- Cook for 7 hours.
- Take two forks and begin to pull the pork roast apart. Shred it and stir thoroughly as you work.
- Cook for an additional hour.
- Serve warm with a side or on a bun.

Nutrition facts per serving (283 g)
Calories: 597
Total fat: 27.0 g.
Carbohydrates: 21.0 g.
Dietary fiber: 1.6 g.
Sugars: 18.4 g.
Protein: 65.3 g.

Spicy Teriyaki Pork Tenderloin

Servings: 8
Preparation time: 20 minutes
Cooking time: 4 hours

Ingredients:

3 lbs of pork tenderloin (3 pork tenderloins)
1 cup of onion slices
4 garlic cloves
3 red chili peppers
2 tbsp of olive oil
1/4 tsp of black pepper
1/4 cup of brown sugar
1/2 cup of teriyaki sauce
1 cup of chicken broth

Directions:

To Prepare for Freezing

- Slice the tenderloins into medallion-sized pieces about a half-inch to an inch thick.
- In a separate bowl, whisk together the chicken broth and teriyaki sauce.
- Fold in the olive oil.
- Measure the brown sugar, and add it to the chicken broth mixture.
- Mince the garlic, and add to the mixture.
- Wash and peel the onion, chop, and add to the mixture.
- Wash and chop the red chili peppers. Add to the mixture.

- Fold in the black pepper and mix the ingredients until they are well blended.
- Place in the pork tenderloin medallions. Stir until the pork is coated.
- Pour into a freezer bag.
- Seal and label the freezer bag with the name of the dish, the date you prepped the meal, the cooking time, and the heat setting.
- Freeze.

To Slow Cook

- Remove from the freezer and run under warm water for 30 seconds or until you have a small amount of liquid in the bag.
- Pour the entire contents of the freezer bag into the slow cooker.
- Set the slow cooker to high and cook for 4 hours. You can also cook it on low for 8 hours.
- Make sure you check the tenderloins every hour and turn them so that they cook evenly.
- Serve warm with rice or other side dish.
- Use the sauce as a gravy.

Nutrition facts per serving (184 g)
Calories: 233
Total fat: 7.7 g.
Carbohydrates: 8.1 g.
Dietary fiber: 0 g.
Sugars: 7.2 g.
Protein: 31.5 g.

VEGETARIAN RECIPES

Want some amazing freezer-to-table recipes without a lot of meat? Look no further than these easy-to-make vegetarian recipes. They are sure to delight everyone in your whole family.

Meatless Sloppy Joes

Servings: 4
Preparation time: 15 minutes
Cooking time: 5 hours

Ingredients:

2 cups of onions
2 garlic cloves
1 cup of green bell peppers
1 cup of red bell peppers
1 3/4 cups of kidney beans (1 -15oz can)
1 tsp of chili powder
2 tbsp of ketchup
1 cup of tomato sauce (1 -8oz can)
1 tbsp of mustard
4 sandwich rolls

Directions:

To Prepare for Freezing

- Wash, peel and chop the onions. Place into a large bowl.
- Mince the garlic, and add to the onions.

- Wash, seed, and chop the green bell peppers, add to the onions.
- Drain and rinse the kidney beans. Add to the vegetable mixture.
- Toss together until it is well blended.
- In a separate bowl, whisk together the ketchup and tomato sauce.
- Fold in the mustard and chili powder. Stir well.
- Pour into the onion and pepper mixture. Mix until the vegetables are coated.
- Transfer to a freezer bag.
- Seal and label the freezer bag with the date you prepped the meal as well as the cooking time and heat setting.Freeze.

To Slow Cook

- Remove the bag from the freezer and run the bag under warm water for a 30 seconds until you have a small amount of liquid in the bag.
- Pour the ingredients into a slow cooker.
- Set the temperature to low, and allow to cook for 5 hours.
- Warm the buns and slice.
- Top the buns with the meatless sloppy Joe mixture.
-

Nutrition facts per serving (336 g)
Calories: 580
Total fat: 8.1 g.
Carbohydrates: 100.5 g.
Dietary fiber: 21.0 g.
Sugars: 15.6 g.
Protein: 28.9 g.

Artichoke Casserole

Servings: 8
Preparation time: 20 minutes
Cooking time: 4 hours

Ingredients:
1 cup of mushrooms
3 green onions
1 3/4 cup of artichoke hearts (1 -14oz can)
2 garlic cloves
2 1/2 cups of fresh spinach
1 tbsp of lemon juice
1 tbsp of butter
2 tbsp of flour, all purpose
1/2 tsp of black pepper
1 1/4 cups of cream of mushroom soup (1 -10oz can)
1 tbsp of fresh parsley
1/4 tsp of Worcestershire sauce
1 cup of sour cream
2 cups of Monterey Jack cheese

Directions:

To Prepare for Freezing

- Wash and chop your mushrooms.
- In a large frying pan, heat the pan and melt the butter.
- Add the mushrooms to the pan.
- Pour in the lemon juice. Stir so the lemon juice coats the mushrooms.
- Fold in the black pepper.
- Mince the garlic, and add to the mushroom mixture.

- Sauté until the mushrooms become tender, about 5 minutes.
- Remove from heat, and cool completely.
- Fill a pot with water, and bring to a bowl.
- Wash the spinach, and then add to the bowling pot of water. Boil for 3 to 5 minutes. Do not overcook the spinach.
- Remove from water and drain. Press the spinach between paper towels, to remove excess moisture.
- Allow to cool completely.
- Place the spinach into a bowl, and add the mushroom soup and sour cream.
- Wash and chop the green onions. Add to the spinach mixture, and stir until it is well blended.
- Drain the artichoke hearts, rinse, and chop. Add to spinach.
- Fold in the flour and Worcestershire sauce.
- Chop the parsley until it is fine, and add to the spinach.
- Add the cooled mushroom mixture to the spinach. Mix thoroughly.
- Transfer the ingredients into a freezer bag.
- Shred the cheese, and place into a separate bag.
- Place both freezer bags into a large freezer bag.
- Seal and label the freezer bag with the name of the dish, the date you prepped the meal, the cooking time, and the heat setting.
- Freeze.

To Slow Cook

- Remove the bag from the freezer.
- Place the cheese into the fridge for later
- Take the mushroom and spinach bag and run the bag under warm water for 30 seconds until you have a small amount of liquid in the bag.
- Pour the ingredients into a slow cooker.
- Set the temperature of the slow cooker to low.
- Cook for 3 hours.
- After 3 hours, take half of the cheese, and stir it into the casserole.
- Sprinkle the remaining cheese on top of the casserole.
- Cook for an additional hour.
- Serve warm.

Nutrition facts per serving (227 g)
Calories: 299
Total fat: 23.0 g.
Carbohydrates: 10.4 g.
Dietary fiber: 1.9 g.
Sugars: 1.2 g.
Protein: 12.7 g.

Bean and Spinach Layered Enchiladas

Servings: 6
Preparation time: 25 minutes
Cooking time: 3 hours

Ingredients:

1 3/4 cups of black beans
2 cups of fresh spinach
1 cup of corn
3 cups of salsa
1/2 cup of sour cream
1 lime, just the juice
1 tsp of cumin
1 tsp of chili powder
1 tsp of coriander
1/2 tsp of salt
1/2 tsp of pepper
1 1/2 cups of cheddar cheese
8 soft tortilla shells

Directions:

To Prepare for Freezing

- Fill a saucepan with water, and bring to a boil on the stove.
- Wash the spinach, and place in the boiling water.
- Cook for 3 to 5 minutes. Remove from water and drain.
- Press excess water out of the spinach by pressing it between two paper towels.
- Place in a bowl.

- In a separate bowl, mix together the cumin, chili powder, and coriander.
- Fold in the salt and pepper.
- Rinse the black beans, and place half in a separate bowl. Mash them until you have a paste.
- Pour the remaining black beans into the spice mixture.
- Fold in the corn and spinach.
- Squeeze the lime, and add the juice to the spinach mixture. Mix well. Pour the mixture into a freezer bag.
- Shred the cheese and place into its own freezer bag.
- Add the paste into a third freezer bag. Seal all of the bags.
- Place all three bags into a larger freezer bag and seal.
- Label the freezer bag with the name of the dish, the date you prepped the meal, the cooking time, and the heat setting.
- Freeze.

To Slow Cook

- Before cooking, remove the bag from the freezer and thaw in the fridge for 24 hours.
- Take a 1/2 cup of salsa and spread it on the bottom of the slow cooker.
- Lay down 1 to 2 tortillas to cover the bottom of the slow cooker.
- Spread a few teaspoons of the black bean paste onto the tortilla.
- Top with a cup of the spinach mixture.
- Add a 1/2 cup of salsa over the spinach mixture.

- Sprinkle a 1/2 cup of cheese over the spinach mixture.
- Top with 1 to 2 tortillas to cover the next layer.
- Repeat with the black bean paste, then the spinach mixture, and then the salsa before you finish with the cheese. Repeat until you have no more tortilla shells and spinach mixture.
- End the final layer with a 1/2 cup of salsa and a 1/2 cup of cheese.
- Set the slow cooker to low, and cook for 3 hours.
- Serve warm, and garnish with sour cream.

Nutrition facts per serving (328 g)
Calories: 546
Total fat: 18.1 g.
Carbohydrates: 72.9 g.
Dietary fiber: 14.7 g.
Sugars: 7.8 g.
Protein: 28.4 g.

Spinach and Ricotta Lasagna

Servings: 6
Preparation time: 15 minutes
Cooking time: 4 hours

Ingredients:

2 1/2 cups of fresh spinach
3 cups of marinara sauce
1 cup of ricotta cheese
1 1/2 cups of mozzarella cheese
3/4 cup of parmesan cheese
6 lasagna noodles

Directions:

To Prepare for Freezing

- Fill a saucepan with water, and bring to a boil on the stove.
- Wash the spinach, and place in the boiling water.
- Cook for 3 to 5 minutes. Remove from water and drain.
- Press excess water out of the spinach by pressing it between two paper towels.
- Place in a large bowl.
- Once the spinach is cool, fold in the ricotta cheese.
- Add 1/2 cup of parmesan cheese. Mix until it is well blended.
- Spoon into a freezer bag and seal.
- In a separate bowl, mix together the water and the marinara sauce.

- Pour into a second freezer bag and seal.
- Shred the mozzarella cheese and place in a third freezer bag before sealing.
- Place all three bags into a large freezer bag.
- Seal and label the freezer bag with the name of the dish, the date you prepped the meal, the cooking time, and the heat setting.
- Freeze.

To Slow Cook

- Before cooking, remove the bag from the freezer, and thaw in the fridge for 24 hours.
- Once it is thawed, start by placing 3/4 cup of the marinara sauce in the bottom of a slow cooker.
- Top that with 2 uncooked lasagna noodles. You may have to use more or break them to make them fit.
- Top the noodles with 3/4 cup of the marinara mixture.
- Add half of the spinach mixture, and spread it across the marinara mixture.
- Cover the spinach with 1/2 cup of mozzarella cheese.
- Top with 2 more uncooked lasagna noodles.
- Top the noodles with 3/4 cup of the marinara mixture.
- Add half of the spinach mixture and spread it across the marinara mixture.
- Cover the spinach with 1/2 cup of mozzarella cheese.
- Top with 2 final uncooked lasagna noodles.

- Cover the noodles with the remaining marinara mixture, and finish with the remaining mozzarella cheese.
- Turn the slow cooker to low, and cook for 4 hours.
- Serve warm.

Nutrition facts per serving (385 g)
Calories: 799
Total fat: 38 g.
Carbohydrates: 58.0 g.
Dietary fiber: 3.5 g.
Sugars: 11.2 g.
Protein: 60.3 g.

Vegetarian Jambalaya

Servings: 8
Preparation time: 20 minutes
Cooking time: 5 hours

Ingredients:

2 cups of vegetarian sausage
1 onion
5 cups of vegetable broth
1 green bell pepper
2 celery stalks
3 scallions
1 3/4 cups of kidney beans (1 -14 oz can)
3 garlic cloves
3 tomatoes
2 tbsp of paprika
1 tsp of dried oregano
2 tbsp of cumin
1 tsp of thyme
1 tsp of black pepper
1 tbsp of olive oil
2 cups of rice, uncooked

Directions:

To Prepare for Freezing

- Wash all the vegetables and peel them. Seed the pepper.
- Chop the onion, bell pepper, and celery stalks.
- Mince the garlic. Put all the vegetables and garlic into a bowl.

- Dice the tomatoes, and add to the vegetable bowl.
- Drain and rinse the kidney beans before adding them to the bowl.
- In a separate bowl, mix together the black pepper, paprika, oregano, cumin, and thyme. Whisk until it is well blended.
- Pour the spices onto the vegetables.
- Add the olive oil, and toss until the vegetables are coated.
- Transfer to a freezer bag.
- Chop the sausage, and place in a separate freezer bag.
- Put both freezer bags into a large freezer bag.
- Seal and label the freezer bag with name of the dish, the date you prepped the meal, the cooking time, and the heat setting.
- Freeze.

To Slow Cook

- Remove from the freezer, and pour the contents of the vegetable bag into a slow cooker. Put the sausage bag in the fridge until you are ready for it.
- Set to low, and cook for 3 hours. Stir the ingredients occasionally.
- After 3 hours, add the rice to the mixture. Blend thoroughly.
- Turn the temperature to high, and cook for another 1½ hours.
- A half hour before it is done, add the sausage bag.
- Cook for 30 minutes.

- Chop the scallions and use the scallions to garnish the dish.
- Serve warm.

Nutrition facts per serving *(356 g)*
Calories: 429
Total fat: 6.0 g.
Carbohydrates: 71.0 g.
Dietary fiber: 10.4 g.
Sugars: 4.2 g.
Protein: 22.5 g.

Sweet and Spice Vegetarian Curry

Servings: 6
Preparation time: 30 minutes
Cooking time: 6 hours

Ingredients:
1/3 of a head of cabbage
1 sweet potato
1 onion
1/2 can of chick peas
1 apple
4 celery stalks
1/2 cup of carrots
2 1/2 cups of vegetable broth
2 tbsp of olive oil
1 tsp of garlic powder
1 tsp of cinnamon
1 tsp of curry powder
1 tsp of cayenne pepper
1/2 tsp of salt
1/2 tsp of pepper
1/2 can of light coconut milk

Directions:

To Prepare for Freezing

- Wash and peel your vegetables.
- Chop the celery stalks, carrots, and onion.
- Core and peel the apple, and chop it into bite-sized pieces.
- Peel the sweet potato, and chop into bite-sized pieces.
- Shred the cabbage.

- Combine all the vegetables and toss.
- Rinse the chick peas and add to the vegetables.
- In a separate bowl, combine together the cinnamon, garlic powder, cayenne pepper, salt, pepper, and curry powder.
- Pour onto the vegetables, and toss until the spices coat the vegetables.
- Add the olive oil, and stir until it is well blended.
- Transfer to a freezer bag.
- Seal and label the freezer bag with the name of the dish, the date you prepped the meal, the cooking time, and the heat setting.
- Freeze.

To Slow Cook

- Remove the bag from the freezer.
- Pour the ingredients into a slow cooker.
- Set the temperature to low, and allow to cook for 5 hours.
- After 6 hours, pour in the coconut milk. Stir thoroughly.
- Cook for 15 minutes before serving.
- Serve warm over rice.

Nutrition facts per serving (235 g)
Calories: 117
Total fat: 5.4 g.
Carbohydrates: 14.6 g.
Dietary fiber: 3.6 g.
Sugars: 7.6 g.
Protein: 3.4 g.

SOUPS AND CHILI RECIPES

Warm up on cold days, or simply enjoy these as an appetizer. These soups and chilies are easy to make and even easier to eat.

Green Chili Pork Stew

Servings: 6
Preparation time: 20 minutes
Cooking time: 8 hours

Ingredients:

2 lbs of pork loin, boneless
3 garlic cloves
1 red onion
1 large potato
3 cups of tomatoes
2 cups of green chili peppers
1 tbsp of cumin
2 tsp of oregano
1/8 tsp of cayenne pepper
2 tsp of fresh cilantro
1/4 tsp of salt
1/4 tsp of pepper
2 cups of beef broth
1/4 cup of masa harina

Directions:

To Prepare for Freezing

- Cut the pork loin into 1 inch cubes.
- Place in a bowl, and add the masa harina to the meat.
- Toss the meat until it is coated.
- Heat the oil in a large frying pan until it is bubbling.
- Add the pork and cook until it is browned, usually between 8 to 10 minutes.
- Remove from heat, and allow the pork to cool completely.
- Wash, peel, and chop the potato and onion.
- Place in a separate bowl.
- Wash and dice the tomatoes. Add to the onion mixture.
- Chop the green chili peppers, and toss with the onion mixture.
- Fold in the cumin, garlic, oregano, cayenne pepper, salt, black pepper, and cilantro.
- Mince the garlic, and add to the onion mixture.
- Pour in the beef broth, and mix the ingredients until they are well blended.
- Toss in the pork and stir.
- Transfer the ingredients to a freezer bag.
- Seal and label the freezer bag with name of the dish, the date you prepped the meal, the cooking time, and the heat setting.
- Freeze.

To Slow Cook

- Remove the bag from the freezer. Pour the ingredients into a slow cooker.
- Set the temperature to low, and allow to cook for 8 hours or until the meat is tender.
- Serve warm.

Nutrition facts per serving (406 g)
Calories: 512
Total fat: 8.2 g.
Carbohydrates: 29.2 g.
Dietary fiber: 7.0 g.
Sugars: 8.6 g.
Protein: 47.1 g.

Chunky Beef Stew

Servings: 8
Preparation time: 15 minutes
Cooking time: 8 hours

Ingredients:

1 lb of stewing beef (or a chuck steak or roast as an alternative)
1 onion
2 cups of frozen peas
2 cups of frozen corn
2 cups of frozen carrots
2 cups of frozen green beans
2 medium potatoes
3 cups of tomato juice
2 cups of beef broth
3 tbsp of beef bouillon
1/4 cup of ketchup
1/2 tsp of pepper

Directions:

To Prepare for Freezing

- Cut the stewing beef into 1-inch cubes.
- Place into a large bowl.
- Wash, peel, and chop the potatoes into 1 inch cubes. Toss with the stewing beef.
- Wash, peel, and cut the onion into small pieces. Add to the meat and potatoes.
- Pour in the corn, peas, green beans, and carrots. Toss the meat and vegetables until they are well blended.

- In a separate bowl, whisk together the tomato juice and beef broth.
- Add the beef bouillon and whisk until it is dissolved.
- Fold in the ketchup and pepper, and continue mixing until the ingredients are well blended.
- Pour over the beef and vegetables. Stir until they are coated.
- Transfer to a freezer bag.
- Seal and label the freezer bag with the name of the dish, the date you prepped the meal, the cooking time, and the heat setting.
- Freeze.

To Slow Cook

- Remove the bag from the freezer, and pour the ingredients into a slow cooker.
- Set the temperature to low, and allow to cook for 8 hours.
- Serve warm.

Nutrition facts per serving (416 g)
Calories: 263
Calories from Fat: 40
Total fat: 4.4 g.
Carbohydrates: 33.6 g.
Dietary fiber: 6.7 g.
Sugars: 11.1 g.
Protein: 24.1 g.

Brunswick Stew

Servings: 8
Preparation time: 25 minutes
Cooking time: 6 hours

Ingredients:

1 1/2 lbs of chicken, boneless and skinless
3/4 lb of ground beef
3/4 lb of ground pork
1/2 tbsp of olive oil
1/4 cup of celery
1/2 cup of onion
2 3/4 cups of cream corn (2 - 10oz cans)
1/2 cup of green bell pepper
2 3/4 cups of diced tomatoes, canned (2 - 10oz cans)
1/4 cup of hickory flavored BBQ sauce
1/2 cup of ketchup

Directions:

To Prepare for Freezing

- In a large frying pan, heat the oil until it is bubbling.
- Wash, peel, and chop the onions.
- Wash and chop the celery.
- Add these vegetables to the frying pan, and sauté until they are tender, usually about 10 minutes.
- Chop the chicken into bite-sized pieces, and add to the mixture. Cook until the chicken is almost brown.

- Fold in the pork and beef, and fry until all of the meat is brown.
- Remove from heat, but do not drain. Instead, place in a bowl to allow to cool.
- Once it is cooled to room temperature, add the ketchup and tomatoes to the meat. Mix thoroughly.
- Fold in the BBQ sauce.
- Wash and seed the bell pepper. Add to the meat mixture.
- Transfer to the freezer bag.
- Seal and label the freezer bag with the name of the dish, the date you prepped the meal, the cooking time, and the heat setting.
- Freeze.

To Slow Cook

- Remove the bag from the freezer, and pour the ingredients into a slow cooker.
- Set the temperature to low, and allow to cook for 5 hours.
- After five hours, add the cream corn to the soup, and stir until well blended.
- Continue cooking for an additional hour.
- Serve warm.

Nutrition facts per serving (345 g)
Calories: 389
Total fat: 8.1 g.
Carbohydrates: 25.1 g.
Dietary fiber: 2.4 g.
Sugars: 10.7 g.
Protein: 50.2 g.

Southwestern Chicken Chili

Servings: 6
Preparation time: 15 minutes
Cooking time: 8 hours

Ingredients:

1 1/4 lbs of chicken, boneless and skinless
1 cup of onions
3 garlic cloves
1 green bell pepper
1 3/4 cups of pinto beans (1 - 15oz cans)
1 3/4 cups of diced tomatoes (1 - 14oz can)
1 3/4 cups of picante sauce (1 - 16oz can)
1 tsp of cumin
2 tbsp of chili powder
1/2 tsp of salt
3 tsp of oregano

Directions:

To Prepare for Freezing

- Cut the chicken into 1-inch cubes. Place in a bowl
- Add the cornmeal, oregano, chili powder, salt, and cumin to the bowl with the chicken.
- Toss until the spices are blended, and the chicken is cooked.
- Spoon into a freezer bag and seal.
- In a large bowl, mix together the tomatoes and picante sauce.
- Wash and peel the onions. Chop.

- Wash and seed the bell pepper, chop. You want both the onions and bell pepper to have a fine chop but not be diced.
- Mince the garlic, and add to the picante sauce mixture.
- Add the onion and bell pepper to the sauce.
- Drain and rinse the pinto beans. Add to the sauce mixture.
- Stir until the vegetables are coated.
- Transfer to a second freezer bag.
- Place both bags into a larger freezer bag.
- Seal and label the freezer bag with the name of the dish, the date you prepped the meal, the cooking time, and the heat setting.
- Freeze.

To Slow Cook

- Remove the bag from the freezer.
- Place the chicken at the bottom of the slow cooker.
- Top with the sauce mixture.
- Set the temperature to low, and allow to cook for 8 hours. Stir occasionally so the spices are dispersed throughout the chili.
- Serve warm.

Nutrition facts per serving (309 g)
Calories: 393
Total fat: 4.5 g.
Carbohydrates: 45.9 g.
Dietary fiber: 11.7 g.
Sugars: 6.3 g.
Protein: 41.6 g.

Mom's Chili

Servings: 6
Preparation time: 45 minutes
Cooking time: 6 hours

Ingredients:

2 lbs of ground beef, lean
2 medium cooking onions
6 garlic cloves
1 red bell pepper
1/4 cup of pickled jalapenos
3 3/4 cups of kidney beans (2 – 15 oz cans)
3 1/2 cups of diced tomatoes (1 – 28 oz can)
1 3/4 cups of tomato sauce (1 – 14 oz can)
3 tbsp of vegetable oil
1/4 cup of chili powder
1 tbsp of cumin
1 1/2 tsp of salt

Garnish (optional):
1 cup of cheddar cheese, shredded
1/4 cup of sliced scallions
1 cup of sour cream

Directions:

To Prepare for Freezing

- In a large frying pan, pour in the oil. Heat until it is bubbling.
- Wash, peel, and chop the onions.
- Wash, seed, and chop the bell pepper.
- Place the onions and bell pepper into the hot oil.

- Fry until the vegetables are soft, usually between 5 to 8 minutes.
- Mince the garlic, and add to the pan.
- Mix in the chili powder and cumin, and stir until all of the ingredients are coated in the spices.
- Continue to cook for another minute.
- Once you can smell the spices, add the ground beef and the salt to the frying pan.
- Cook until the ground beef is brown, about 7 to 10 minutes.
- When cooked, remove from heat and cool completely.
- In a large bowl, mix together the diced tomatoes, with their juice, and tomato sauce.
- Drain and rinse the kidney beans. Add to the tomatoes.
- Chop the jalapenos and add to the tomatoes.
- Stir until the ingredients are blended thoroughly.
- Fold in the cooled beef mixture. Stir until the meat is coated.
- Transfer to a freezer bag.
- Seal and label the freezer bag with the name of the dish, the date you prepped the meal, the cooking time, and the heat setting.
- Freeze.

To Slow Cook

- Remove the bag from the freezer, and pour the ingredients into a slow cooker.
- Set the temperature to low, and allow to cook for 6 hours.
- If you like, garnish with the cheese, scallions, or sour cream.

- Serve warm.

Nutrition facts per serving (504 g)
Calories: 811
Total fat: 19.2 g.
Carbohydrates: 86.8 g.
Dietary fiber: 22.8 g.
Sugars: 10.5 g.
Protein: 75.0 g.

Meatless Chili

Servings: 4
Preparation time: 20 minutes
Cooking time: 8 hours

Ingredients:

1 zucchini
1 onion
2 carrots
1 red bell pepper
1 yellow bell pepper
1 1/2 cups of frozen corn
2 1/2 cups of mushrooms
2 1/2 cups of diced tomatoes
1 1/2 tbsp of chili powder
1/2 tsp of red pepper flakes
1/8 tsp of cayenne pepper
1 tsp of Tabasco sauce
1 tsp of cumin
1/2 cup of water
2 1/2 cups of kidney beans (2 - 10 oz cans)

Directions:

To Prepare for Freezing

- Wash, peel, and chop the zucchini. Place into a bowl.
- Wash and seed the red and yellow bell peppers. Chop and add to the bowl with the zucchini.
- Wash, peel, and chop the onion and carrots. Add to the veggie mixture.

- Wash and chop the mushrooms. Add to the zucchini mixture.
- Add the corn, and toss the vegetables.
- Drain and rinse the kidney beans. Toss with the vegetables. Set aside.
- In a separate bowl, combine together the red pepper flakes, chili powder, cayenne pepper and cumin.
- Add the water and Tabasco sauce.
- Wash and dice the tomatoes. Add to the spice mixture.
- Mix until the ingredients are well blended.
- Pour into the vegetable mixture, and stir until the vegetables are coated with the tomato mixture.
- Spoon into a large freezer bag and seal.
- Seal and label the freezer bag with the name of the dish, the date you prepped the meal, the cooking time, and the heat setting.
- Freeze.

To Slow Cook
- Remove the bag from the freezer, and pour the ingredients into a slow cooker.
- Set the temperature to low and allow to cook for 8 hours.
- Serve warm.

Nutrition facts per serving (511 g)
Calories: 523
Total fat: 2.8 g.
Carbohydrates: 99.4 g.
Dietary fiber: 24.6 g.
Sugars: 13.7 g.
Protein: 31.7 g.

Hot and Sour Soup

Servings: 4
Preparation time: 15 minutes
Cooking time: 8 hours

Ingredients:

2 cups of tofu
8 shiitake mushrooms
1 1/4 cups of white mushrooms, sliced
2 tbsp of grated ginger
2 tbsp of vegetable bouillon
4 garlic cloves
1 cup of canned bamboo shoots
1 1/2 cups of frozen peas
1 tsp of chili paste
2 tbsp of soy sauce
4 cups of water
2 tbsp of apple cider vinegar

Directions:

To Prepare for Freezing

- Wash and remove the stems of the mushrooms. Chop into bite-sized pieces. Place in a bowl.
- Mince the garlic cloves, and add to the mushrooms.
- Rinse the bamboo shoots, and chop into bite-sized pieces. Add to the mushrooms.
- Chop the tofu, and add to the mushrooms.
- Toss together before transferring to a freezer bag. Seal.

- In a separate bowl, whisk together the water, soy sauce, and bouillon.
- Whisk in the sesame oil and vinegar.
- Grate the ginger, and add 1 tablespoon to the sesame mixture.
- Add the chili paste to the mixture, and stir until the ingredients are well blended.
- Pour into a separate freezer bag and seal.
- Combine the remaining grated ginger with the peas and mix. Place in a third freezer bag.
- Put the ingredients bag into a larger freezer bag.
- Seal and label the freezer bag with the name of the dish, the date you prepped the meal, the cooking time, and the heat setting.
- Freeze.

To Slow Cook

- Remove the bags from the freezer.
- Empty all but the pea bag into the slow cooker, and set the temperature to low.
- Store the peas in the fridge until you need them.
- Cook for 8 hours.
- About 15 minutes before serving, add the peas to the soup and stir thoroughly.
- Serve warm as an appetizer or meal.

Nutrition facts per serving (664 g)

Calories: 253
Total fat: 6.3 g.
Carbohydrates: 37.3 g.
Dietary fiber: 9.0 g.
Sugars: 10.9 g.
Protein: 18.4 g.

CONCLUSION

I want to thank you for downloading and reading this book. I hope you have enjoyed these slow cooker recipes. The main objective of this book was to make your life easier, and I sincerely hope it has done that for you.

As you can see, the recipes are endless when you are coming up with freezer-to-table dinner ideas. They are fast, can be done in bulk quantities, and most are as simple as adding the ingredients to a slow cooker and walking away until it is done.

Throughout the book, the focus was on ease, and great taste. These healthy recipes can save you money and more importantly, can save you time.

I hope you enjoy the recipes and will be using them for a long time to come!

APPENDIX

<u>*Cooking Conversion Charts*</u>

1. Volumes

US Fluid Oz.	US	US Dry Oz.	Metric Liquid ml
¼ oz.	2 tsp.	1 oz.	10 ml.
½ oz.	1 tbsp.	2 oz.	15 ml.
1 oz.	2 tbsp.	3 oz.	30 ml.
2 oz.	¼ cup	3½ oz.	60 ml.
4 oz.	½ cup	4 oz.	125 ml.
6 oz.	¾ cup	6 oz.	175 ml.
8 oz.	1 cup	8 oz.	250 ml.

Tsp.= teaspoon - tbsp.= tablespoon – oz.= ounce – ml.= millimeter

2. Oven Temperatures

Celsius (ºC)	Fahrenheit (ºF)*
90	220
110	225
120	250
140	275
150	300
160	325
180	350
190	375
200	400
215	425
230	450
250	475
260	500

*Rounded numbers

ABOUT THE AUTHOR

Sarah Spencer lives in Canada with her husband and two children. She describes herself as an avid foodie who prefers watching the Food Network over a hockey game or NCIS! She is a passionate cook who dedicates all her time between creating new recipes, writing cookbooks, and her family, though not necessarily in that order!

Sarah has had two major influences in her life regarding cooking, her Grandmother and Mama Li.

She was introduced to cooking at an early age by her Grandmother who thought cooking for your loved ones was the single most important thing in life. Not only that, but she was the World's Best Cook in the eyes of all those lucky enough to taste her well-kept secret recipes. Over the years, she conveyed her knowledge and appreciation of food to Sarah.

Sarah moved to Philadelphia when her father was transferred there when Sarah was a young teenager. She became close friends with a girl named Jade, whose parents owned a Chinese take-out restaurant.

This is when Sarah met her second biggest influence, Mama Li. Mama Li was Jade's mother and a professional cook in her own restaurant. Sarah would spend many hours in the restaurant as a helper to Mama Li. Her first job was in the restaurant. Mama Li showed Sarah all about cooking Asian food, knife handling, and mixing just the right amount of spices. Sarah became an excellent Asian cook, especially in Chinese and Thai food.

Along the way, Sarah developed her own style in the kitchen. She loves to try new flavors and mix up ingredients in new and innovative ways. She enjoy cooking with her slow cooker and finding ways to make life easier while feeding your loved one with flavorful and healthy meals. She is also very sensitive to her son's allergy to gluten and has been cooking gluten-free and paleo recipes for quite some time.

Some of her other books include: Simple Paleo Salad Cookbook; Best Wok Recipes from Mamma Li's Kitchen; Best Egg Rolls, Spring Rolls and Dumplings from Mama Li's Kitchen, Gluten-Free Today 36 Quick & Easy Lunch and Snack Recipes; Freezer Meals for the Slow Cooker; Totally Thai: Classic Thai Recipes to Make at Home, Thanksgiving Feast Cookbook and Christmas Feast Cookbook.

CPSIA information can be obtained at www.ICGtesting.com
Printed in the USA
LVOW07s1500160116

470958LV00019B/1163/P